IMAGES

of America

GLENVIEW

Pictured is the Glenview Area Historical Society's 1864 Farmhouse Museum, which was originally home to the Hutchings family, among Northfield Township's earliest settlers. The Farmhouse Museum is a local landmark.

On the cover: The dedication of the bear fountain on September 15, 1917, was the greatest event the town had ever seen. The celebration included a parade down Church Street; the Methodist church is visible in the background. (Courtesy of the Glenview Area Historical Society.)

IMAGES
of America

GLENVIEW

Beverly Roberts Dawson

ARCADIA
PUBLISHING

Published by Arcadia Publishing
Charleston, South Carolina

Library of Congress Catalog Card Number: 2007939836

For all general information contact Arcadia Publishing at:
Telephone 843-853-2070
Fax 843-853-0044
E-mail sales@arcadiapublishing.com
For customer service and orders:
Toll-Free 1-888-313-2665

Visit us on the Internet at www.arcadiapublishing.com

*This book is dedicated to the citizens of Glenview—past,
present, and future. It is also for Avery Dawson, Evan O'Brien,
and Emma Dawson, who, although not village residents,
think it is a very cool place to visit.*

CONTENTS

ACKNOWLEDGMENTS

Deepest gratitude goes to Dr. Bill Dawson for the long hours spent scanning photos which made this book possible. Great appreciation is extended to professor Susan Dawson-O'Brien for her expertise in reviewing the contents herein. To Arcadia editor Jeff Ruetsche—many thanks for his patience and guidance. Countless Glenview residents contributed their stories: Bob Coffin, Joyce Dug Hutchings, Don and Mary Long, Mary Meizer, Norma Morrison, Sharon Burke Siegel, Mary Jane Stevens, Dick Zander, and Warren Ziegler were most helpful. Special thanks to Glenview Area Historical Society's superb researchers—Marge Marcquenski, Dorothy Murphy, Virginia Peterson, and Norman Carlson. Finally, those who founded and maintained the Glenview Area Historical Society for the past 40 years deserve recognition; without their efforts, Glenview's history might have been lost completely. The late Jean Voght especially must be remembered as one whose knowledge and devotion contributed greatly to the society's success.

Unless otherwise noted, all photographs contained in this book are from the archives of the Glenview Area Historical Society. In years past, three major books were written to chronicle the village's history: *Glenview 1899–1974* (compiled by Alice Head and Clare Benepe), *Roots: A Glenview Story* (edited by Isabel Ernst), and *Glenview: The First Centennial* (published by Paul H. Thomas). Because these volumes contain a great deal of information about the village in the latter years of the 20th century, this volume concentrates upon the arrival of the first Europeans and continues through the first 70 years following incorporation. Due to space limitations, this is but a brief overview of a much larger story. When researching history, conflicting information is to be found at every turn; great effort has been made to verify and document the material herein.

INTRODUCTION

"Our future rests on our past"; this quotation from newspaperman Sydney J. Harris succinctly sums up a major reason for preserving history. The earliest records of exploration of the area that now includes the village of Glenview go back to the 17th century. Native Americans—tribes of the Potawatomi—were known to have occupied several villages in the area. What is less well known is just when the first European explorers paddled canoes up the west fork of the north branch of the Chicago River. A 1955 history by A. E. Gyllenhaal, respected writer, newspaper editor, amateur historian, and resident of Swedenborg Park, states that the French explorer Jean Nicolet was the first person to explore this region, about 1635. Nicolet's journey began in 1634, following a route from Montreal, through the St. Lawrence River, through the Great Lakes to the Menominee River at Marinette, Wisconsin, then via the Wisconsin River, and finally into Illinois by way of the Des Plaines River. His party portaged its canoes to the south branch of the Chicago River to Lake Michigan. Nicolet's diary noted Grosse Pointe (which he called "Beauty's Eyebrow"), the current location of the Evanston's Grosse Pointe Lighthouse. From there, the party went on to explore the north branch, with its various forks or tributaries.

According to Gyllenhaal's detailed account, Louis Jolliet and Fr. Jacques Marquette's exploration followed Nicolet's route in 1673. They paddled up the Chicago River south of what is now Golf Road but could not continue up the east fork due to ice. They were, however, able to travel up the west fork to what they called the "Indian log bridge" where today's Waukegan Road crosses the river.

Early visitors discovered a marshy, sometimes swampy terrain with prairie grass surrounding occasional groves of trees. On what high ground was to be found, Native Americans established trails on roads now named Milwaukee, Sunset Ridge, and Glenview. The Native Americans portaged their canoes between the Des Plaines River and Lake Michigan. The trails were lined by saplings bent to mark the way; very few of these trees exist today.

Prior to the Treaty of 1833, which specified that Native Americans living in the region be relocated (most of them west of the Mississippi River), a number of European homesteaders settled around present-day Glenview. An acre of land cost $1.25 (by 1850, the price skyrocketed to about $13 per acre). Among these immigrants were John Dewes and his family; they arrived about 1825 and farmed their land for nearly 75 years. The property was purchased by the Glen View Golf and Polo Club in 1897; the Dewes family moved farther west to the hamlet of Glen View. Some other original settlers were veterans of the War of 1812; they were rewarded with land grants for their military service.

Prior to the chartering of Northfield Township, the area had no identity of its own and was simply part of Cook County. Sgt. Joseph Adams mustered out of the army at Fort Dearborn and established a rudimentary trading post near the present intersection of Glenview and Waukegan Roads about 1833. His neighbors were Benjamin Toops and Dardenus Bishop, who purchased tracts of land nearby. They are the first documented residents of the future village of Glenview.

When Northfield Township was established in 1850, it was divided into three districts: North Northfield (later Shermerville, now Northbrook), South Northfield (now Glenview), and West Northfield (now incorporated into Glenview). Northfield Township's leaders were a supervisor, a town clerk, an assessor, a tax collector, a poormaster, two justices of the peace, two constables, and three highway commissioners. The highway commissioners apparently set to work at once, as a dirt road then called State Road (later Lake Street, then Glenview Road) was built about 1854. It extended from Milwaukee Avenue to the middle of present downtown Glenview. It was expanded east from Little Fort Trail (later Mill Street, then Waukegan Road) to Ridge Avenue in Wilmette in 1856.

The South Northfield district was located upon the floodplain for the west fork of the north branch of the Chicago River. To this neighborhood came Hutchingses, Rugens, Appleyards, Sesterhenns, Reeds, Hoffmans, Heslingtons, Melzers, and Claveys. By 1840, the need for a school for their children was recognized, and a makeshift classroom was situated in a cooper's (barrel maker's) shop. Julia Grote was hired as the teacher; her salary was $1.50 per week. A post office, designated South Northfield, operated from 1853 to 1880. Another, named North Branch, was established in 1871. The name was changed to Oak Glen in 1878 and Glen View in 1895. Thus the district had two coexisting postal addresses for about nine years during the 1870s.

As towns and villages developed, their perimeters did not strictly follow township boundaries. Today, while most of the village of Glenview lies within Northfield Township, portions are situated in Maine, New Trier, and Niles Townships. This still creates complications for the village's school, library, and park districts.

In 1836, Dr. John Kennicott brought his family from New Orleans to settle in West Northfield, along the old Milwaukee Trace (now Milwaukee Avenue). A rudimentary route for stagecoaches (actually little more than boxy wagons) was initiated along the road between Chicago and Milwaukee that same year. Other Kennicott family members joined John and family; the area grew to include the Sherwins, Dearloves, and Allisons. Their post office, designated the Grove, was established in 1848; Dr. John Kennicott was its first postmaster. Ten postmasters would follow him over the next 50 years, until the post office closed for good in 1901.

By the beginning of the 20th century, the swampy area upon which early Glenview businesses and residences were built was called "frog town"; it extended north to present-day Glenview Road, west to the railroad tracks, east to Waukegan Road, and south to the Carriage Hill townhomes. Some owners of houses along Glenview Road, as well as Dewes and Prairie Streets, had to build small wooden bridges between their residences and the street. The village's own "White City" (reflecting the color of its homes) extended west of the railroad tracks and south of Glenview Road.

Chicago's Great Fire of 1871 had a profound effect on all of Northfield Township. Cinders from the fire had barely cooled when the intrepid residents of Chicago rolled up their sleeves and began to rebuild. The forests of Wisconsin supplied much of the lumber for the job.

To transport building materials, the Chicago, Milwaukee, St. Paul and Pacific Railroad laid its first set of tracks along a route that ran directly through South Northfield; the hamlet was now connected to the outside world. The age of rail travel shifted population growth from the old stagecoach routes along Milwaukee in West Northfield to neighboring South Northfield. In 1898, the founding fathers gave the community its current name. Originally two words (Glen View), the name finally evolved into Glenview toward the end of the 1920s.

One

SOUTH NORTHFIELD

The first European settlers coexisted in this area with local Potawatomi Indian tribes. In 1833, Sgt. Joseph Adams, the last enlisted man at Fort Dearborn, retired from the army and brought his wife, Hannah, and their family upriver to establish a farm and trading post along the banks of the west fork of the north branch of the Chicago River. They lived here until his demise in 1885. Ever wet and often swampy, the land was a challenge even for those hardy early residents. The Hutchings family, who homesteaded the land where downtown Glenview is now located, arrived in 1843. By 1860, there were many well-established farms in the area; they provided food for the Union army and the area citizens prospered. St. Peter Evangelical Lutheran Church was built on Telegraph Road (now Shermer Avenue) in 1863; the church burned about 100 years later but the old churchyard cemetery remains at the site. By the 1890s, railroad transportation was well established; trains made it possible for commuters to work in Chicago and live in the country. Among the commuters were members of the Swedenborg community who moved here to establish their homes; many of these residents were among the district's initial "movers and shakers." A second set of tracks was laid in 1892 to accommodate the trains which would carry huge numbers of passengers to the 1893 Columbian Exposition in Chicago. In 1896, when the first telephone in the district was installed in John Lies' Saloon, the hamlet moved rapidly into the age of technology.

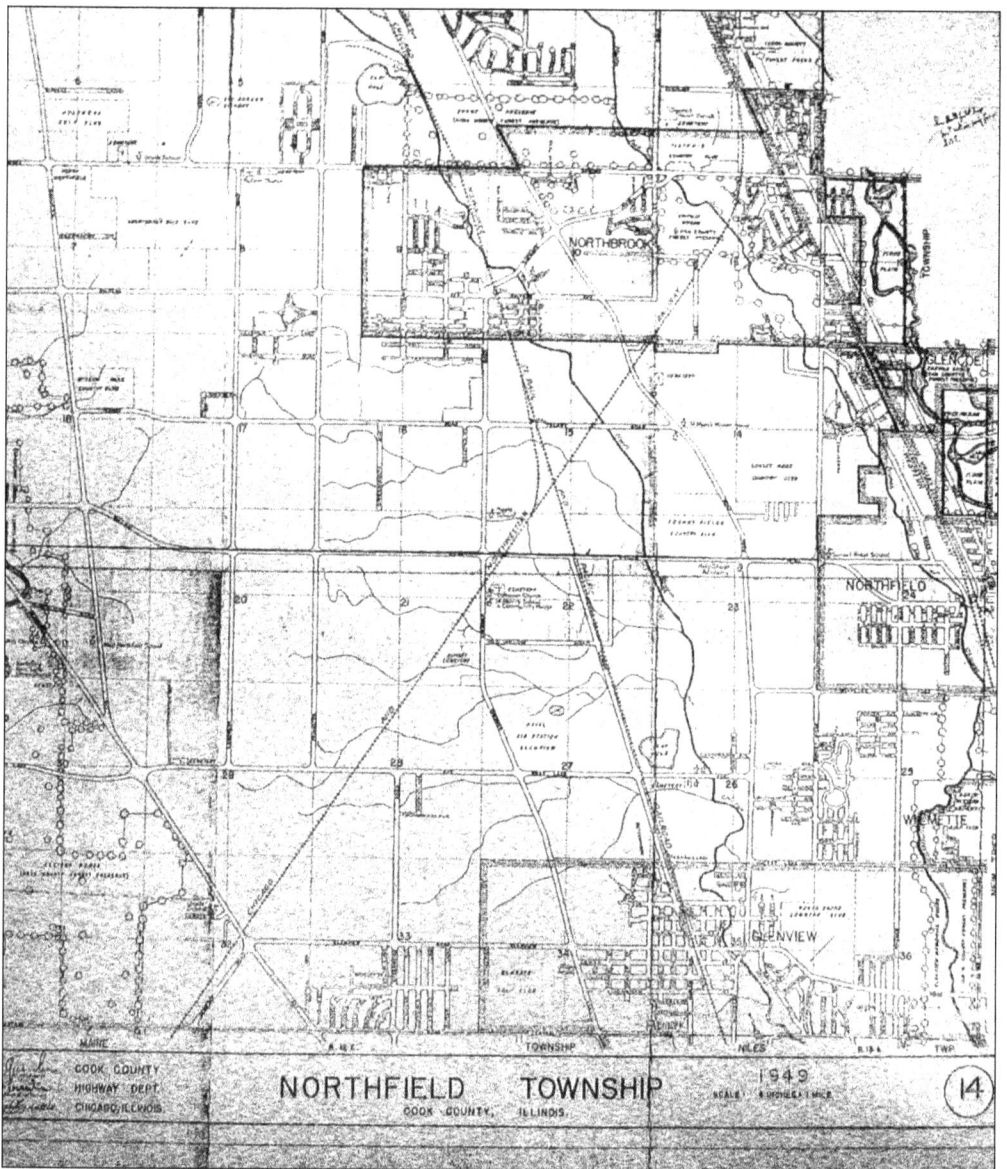

Northfield Township was established on April 2, 1850. Within its approximately 35 square miles lie the present-day villages of Glenview, Northbrook, and most of Northfield. The first European settlers arrived in the area some 20 years before the township was formed and had already homesteaded large acreages. Those who settled in the southern portion of the township called the area South Northfield.

Much of the land was boggy and prone to flooding. This created serious challenges for homesteaders as they endeavored to build homes and grow crops. A history written by Glenview resident A. E. Gylenhaal indicates that Louis Jolliet and Fr. Jacques Marquette noted a Native American bridge was located where the north branch passes under present-day Waukegan Road. A stone bridge was built over the river in 1902.

Sarah Linden Hutchings, along with her husband, James, emigrated from England in 1843 and established a homestead on land that later became Glenview's downtown. James, like many of his neighbors in South Northfield, caught gold fever in 1849. A group from the district banded together to seek its fortunes in California. Before construction of the transcontinental railroad, the arduous and risky route to the West Coast was down the Mississippi River to New Orleans and from there by ship to Central America. In Panama, James contracted another kind of fever—yellow fever—and died. Sarah remained in South Northfield with their five children and kept the farm going. While two of her sons, John and William, were serving in the Union army during the Civil War, she built the family homestead, which, nearly 100 years later, became the Glenview Area Historical Society's Farmhouse Museum.

The Hutchings boys returned to Glenview when the war was over and built a gristmill and sawmill across from the family home. Local farmers brought grain to be ground into flour or cornmeal and trees to make lumber. As Glenview developed, portions of the farm were sold off for homes and businesses.

An old Native American trail, known as the Milwaukee Trace, became a main route between Chicago and Milwaukee. The area was known as West Northfield and much later became part of Glenview. In 1836, Dr. John Kennicott moved his family here from New Orleans. Their first home was a modest log cabin; this more spacious residence was constructed in 1856. In addition to his medical practice, he established the Grove Nursery, which ultimately led to the founding of Chicago's Kennicott Brothers Company in 1881. It was the first wholesale florist business in the Midwest, and the company is now one of the oldest ongoing businesses in Illinois. Through the diligence of a devoted band of women (called the Fern and Frog Ladies), the Grove became a national landmark in 1973.

Robert Kennicott, a son of Dr. John and Mary Kennicott, was born the year before the family settled at the Grove. He inherited his parents' fascination for nature and spent his youth studying the plants and animals that surrounded his home. As a young man, Robert became a naturalist. His association with the Smithsonian Institution (beginning in 1853) was instrumental in the founding of the Chicago Academy of Sciences in 1856. Health problems plagued him all his life, and he died while on an expedition to Alaska 10 years later. His work there contributed to the decision that led to the United States' purchase of Alaska from Russia in 1867.

Settlers along Milwaukee Avenue soon felt the need to build a school for the growing number of children in the district. Dr. John Kennicott took the lead in organizing the Grove School. Designed by a Chicago architect and built at a cost of $400, the structure could accommodate 36 children. With Cordelia Boyden as teacher, the school opened its doors to the first scholars in 1854.

South of the Grove on Milwaukee Avenue was the M. C. Sherwin farm and the Stagecoach Tavern. The tavern, built around 1840, included a small hotel for travelers. The property was sold to the Sudyam family about 1867. High water and mud were perennial problems for both humans and horses. One early attempt to solve the dilemma came in the form of a wooden plank road, depicted here in front of the tavern. The fee for use of the road was expensive—$1.30 for the Chicago-to-Wheeling portion. These roads were short-lived; a lack of drainage resulted in decay, and planks floated away during heavy rains. After World War II, the Nelson Printing Company occupied the old tavern property for nearly 50 years. At the time the building was demolished, it was one of the oldest buildings in Cook County.

GLENVIEW.

C.M.& ST.P. R.R. STA. GLENVIEW. PUB.

Chicago's Great Fire of 1871 brought rapid change to South Northfield. Rebuilding of the city began almost immediately, and railroads expanded rapidly to accommodate necessary transport of building materials, especially lumber from northern forests. The Chicago, Milwaukee, St. Paul and Pacific Railroad laid its first set of tracks in 1872 along a route that ran through the village. Now connected to the larger world, the village prospered. For a time, an old boxcar served as a railroad station. Later a wood frame station served the village for about 70 years until it was demolished.

Al Eustis, a retired railroad man, built this tavern in 1878. Ideally situated next to the railroad and on one of the village's main roads, Lake Street (now Glenview Road), its patrons included local residents and travelers alike. Hotel rooms were located upstairs, with a saloon on the ground floor. It has undergone alterations over the years and a name change or two, but it looks today much as it did originally. This venerable brick building, now called the Glenview House, is the oldest commercial building still standing in Glenview.

After Herman Rugen's first wife, Henrietta Schwinge Rugen, died, he married her sister Katrina. The couple and their two sons emigrated from Germany in 1852. They settled in South Northfield and had three more children. Again widowed, Herman married the third Schwinge sister, Anna; together they had eight children. Herman operated a store from the living room of the Rugen home beginning in 1869. The business flourished and soon outgrew the original space. Herman and his son Charles built this general store and cheese factory at Telegraph Road (now Shermer Avenue) and Lake Avenue in 1876. In 1891, the Rugen store moved to Oak Glen. C. D. Rugen and Henry Appleyard formed a partnership and operated the Rugen and Appleyard store in a building formerly owned by John Hutchings.

One of the oldest ongoing churches in Glenview was founded in 1876. The Evangelical Immanuel Lutheran Church was dedicated in June of that year. The original church, along with its churchyard cemetery, was located on the south side present-day Chestnut Avenue. The current church, dedicated in 1926, was built on the north side of the road.

Sarah Linden Hutchings donated land on Church Street in 1885 for Glenview's Methodist church. The "little white church" remained at that location for 68 years, until the congregation bought several acres on Harlem Avenue. A new church was dedicated in 1953; additions to the original structure were built over the next 20 years.

The Appleyards, one of Glenview's founding families, pose for a formal portrait dated 1893. Richard Appleyard homesteaded land where the Glenview Park District golf course now stands. In 1855, he was a founder of the Christian Brotherhood Church and donated land for construction of the small house of worship. In 1894, the building was purchased by Alfred and Amanda Goerwitz and moved to Swedenborg Park, where they converted it into a residence. The house has undergone extensive changes but is still occupied today.

One of the North Shore's first planned communities was formed in Oak Glen in 1894. Members of the Swedenborg Society in Chicago relocated to find a healthier environment in which to raise their families. They built homes and a clubhouse on 40 acres of farmland purchased from August Clavey. Their clubhouse included space for a school, which opened with 20 pupils that autumn. The original building burned to the ground in 1915; the community rebuilt and dedicated the Immanuel Church of the New Jerusalem in 1916.

This orchestra, composed of members of the New Church, included several noteworthy gentlemen. Members are, from left to right, (first row) John B. Synnestvedt, Louis Riefstahl, Seymour G. Nelson, Rev. N. D. Pendleton, Alvin E. Nelson, and Jesse A. Burt; (second row) William H. Junge, Felix E. Boericke, and Hugh L. Burnham. Synnestvedt and the Nelsons were members of families who owned nurseries in the village. Pendleton was pastor of the New Church. Burnham, a nephew of famed Chicago architect Daniel Burnham, served as the village's first mayor. Burt was associated with Chicago's Field Museum; there is some evidence that he may have engineered the first heavier-than-air aircraft in Glenview in the late 1890s.

Daniel Burnham was one of the founders of the Glen View Golf and Polo Club in 1897. Many club members lived in Evanston and Wilmette. A trolley car traveling on tracks down present-day Old Orchard Road, past Harms Road, then on to club property, provided transportation from points east. Other golfers arrived via train, which stopped at the village of Golf station. A nearby livery stable provided horse-drawn transportation to the club.

Two

GLEN VIEW

The town had been called Oak Glen for many years when the railroad required that a new name be adopted to avoid confusion with another Oak Glen on the line south of Chicago. After lively discussion of several potential choices—including Rugenville, Glenvarr, Glendale, Glengrove, Glen Hollow and Oak View—Glen View was adopted in 1895. A first attempt to incorporate as a village failed in 1898 but passed by nine votes in 1899. Had women been entitled to cast a ballot in those years, one can but wonder whether the issue would have passed the first time around, since one of the main issues was the need for sidewalks along the hamlet's muddy streets. Agriculture continued to be the mainstay of local economy. At the dawn of the 20th century, Glen View was official and on its way toward improving life for its taxpayers. The first 20 years following incorporation saw the village's population double, bringing new businesses, churches, schools, and municipal services. In the summer of 1909, the Northwestern Gas Company came to the village, ushering in gaslights for homes and businesses. By 1912, there were concrete sidewalks along Lake Street (now Glenview Road). A water and sewer system was in place by 1916. And in the year prior to America's involvement in World War I, Edwin S. Jackman's gift of the now famous bear fountain provided Glen View with an image that would give the village a landmark as well as its future logo.

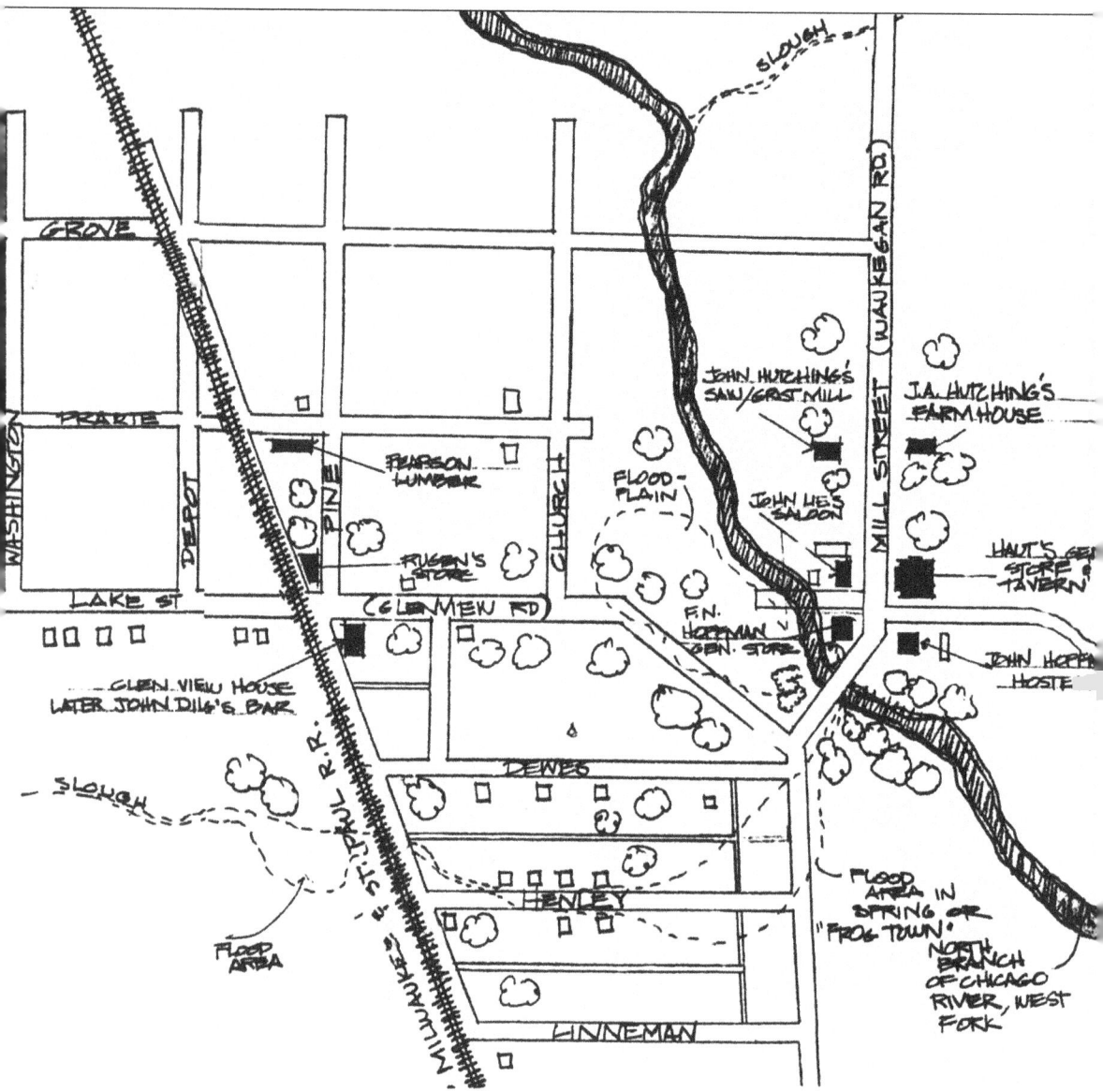

DOWNTOWN GLEN VIEW

CIRCA 1900 A.D.

The late Donald N. Fisk drew this rendition of downtown Glen View as it appeared about 1900. It vividly illustrates the village's location in the middle of the floodplain, as well as locations of businesses of the day.

One of the first homes completed in the Swedenborg community was that of Hugh and Mary Burnham. It was in this handsome residence that they raised 10 children. Hugh, an attorney with law offices in Chicago, was a born leader and served as Glen View's first mayor. He is credited with suggesting the name chosen for the village, based on his observation of the view of the glen from an upstairs window of his home. (At the time, there were few buildings to the east between his home and what became Glenview's downtown; his view was virtually unobstructed.)

John Dilg purchased the former Eustis tavern and added a third story in 1899. Its new look is pictured here on the left, with the new Rugen stores building (built in 1905) on the right. The spacious third floor of Dilg's Tavern was to become a kind of all-purpose meeting hall until a new Glenview Civic Center was constructed 30 years later. Incorporation documents for the village of Glen View were signed at Dilg's on June 20, 1899. Since it was now up to the newly formed municipality to maintain its own law and order, three saloon keepers—John Lies, William Haut, and John Dilg—were appointed the first constables.

And afterwards to wit on the 2nd day of June A. D. 1899 the following among other proceedings were had by and before said Court and entered of record, to wit.

In the matter of the Petition for the incorporation of the Village of Glenview) Order

Now this day this cause coming on to be heard upon the petition this day filed herein, and it appearing to the Court, that the petitioners subscribing said petition are thirty (30) in number; and are each of them legal voters residing within the limits of the territory described in said petition, to wit: Section Thirty-four (34) and Thirty-five (35), (except the East quarter (E¼) thereof) in Township Forty-two (42) North, Range Twelve (12), East of the Third (3rd) Principal Meridian, in the Town of Northfield, County of Cook and State of Illinois; and it further appearing to the Court that said territory is contiguous and does not ex—

The first vote for incorporation fell short of a majority in 1898 but passed in 1899; the required number of votes was 325. Hugh Burnham was elected village president; the first trustees were Henry Maynard, Frank Hoffman, C. D. Rugen, John Hutchings, August Clavey, and A. C. Butzow.

Glen View's early post offices moved frequently. They were usually located within a store, with the store's owner serving as postmaster. Here is the post office when it was located in the Rugen stores from 1913 to 1918. Townspeople collected their mail in person until 1941, when city delivery was initiated.

Those with a rural free delivery (RFD) address depended upon mail carriers and wagons. The service was established about 1900. Bill Rugen made his rounds to the farms surrounding Glen View from 1921 until he retired in 1940.

Taken from the roof of the Rugen stores looking east, this photograph includes a view of Lake Street (now Glenview Road). In the downtown of about 100 years ago, businesses were few and far between.

At the corner of Mill Street (now Waukegan Road) and Lake Street (now Glenview Road) were more saloons. Bill Haut's Place, with its turretlike windows projecting outward, is seen on the right. The building survived until the early 1970s. In the early years of the 20th century, a dance pavilion was located behind the saloon, with music provided by local musicians. The evening was said to be over when the dancers went home or members of the band became inebriated— whichever came first.

This view looking west on what is now Glenview Road provides a perspective of the village's rural roots. It was probably taken late in the second decade of the 20th century; both electric and telephone utility poles are visible along the dirt road. Horsepower was still mostly of the four-legged variety, and chickens were allowed to roam freely along the railroad right-of-way. The white house in the right background still stands at Washington Street and Glenview Road.

In 1889, H. L. Harms built this saloon a block north of Lake Street (now Glenview Road). Leo N. Lang bought the tavern in 1902. When Lang was stuck and killed by a train, his family carried on. Later the Rugen family operated it for about 50 years. Its colorful past includes a period when the upstairs was a popular betting parlor. Its elaborate telephone connections enabled it to function as one of the area's major "bookie joints" in the mid-20th century. Today a restaurant and bar still operates at the original location.

Three-time mayor Horace M. McCullen lived with his family in this home at 1775 Lake Street (now Glenview Road). The village's first telephone exchange was located in the home; Mrs. McCullen served as the telephone operator. Housing medical and dental offices, the Colonial Court building stands at that address today.

The first Our Lady of Perpetual Help Roman Catholic Church was built on land purchased from Sarah Linden Hutchings's son William in 1906. The new brick church was dedicated in November 1907 to serve the growing number of parishioners. Before there was a formal church, the pastor, Fr. Martin Schmidt, celebrated mass on the third floor of John Dilg's Glen View House.

In 1903, the Pearson Lumber Company was located on Pine Street in close proximity to the railroad and was then sold to Edward A. Hines Lumber in 1908. It operated at the site for nearly a century before it was demolished to make way for townhomes.

Around the beginning of the 20th century, the Melzer Funeral Home was located near present-day Greenwood and Glenview Roads. The undertaker built coffins on the premises and prepared the deceased for viewing. In those years, it was customary for the departed one's wake to be in his or her own home. A horse-drawn hearse—a boxy wagon with glass side panels—carried the coffin to a final resting place.

In 1868, Alex Turney bought an acre of William Appleyard's land on the southwest corner of State and Telegraph Roads (now Glenview Road and Shermer Avenue). He paid $100 for the property. In 1896, it was sold and became the Honeman Blacksmith Shop. Fred Buhrke bought the business in 1922 for $2,000 and renamed it the Buhrke Blacksmith and Wagon Shop. The property was passed on to Fred's son, Elmer, who operated the West End Garage at the location until 1952.

John Meizer immigrated to South Northfield from Germany and bought the family home in 1871 (the house was built much earlier). Three generations of the Melzers are pictured here. From left to right are (first row) Lulu and Josephine (Adam's younger daughters); (second row) two Heimgartner children, John Melzer and his wife, Katherine Melzer (Adam's daughter), William Melzer (Adam's son), Louisa Melzer (Adam's wife) and Adam Melzer; (third row) Mrs. Heimgartner (John's niece) holding the hand of her child and Mr. Heimgartner at the far right in front of the cellar entrance.

A landmark along the old Native American trail that became Lake Street (now Glenview Road) was a giant cottonwood tree. Standing 165 feet tall and 18 feet in diameter, it was often referred to as the "Indian Council Tree" or "Pottawatomi Tree." It was located on Big Tree Farm just west of present-day Edens Expressway and north of Glenview Road. About 1900, its age was assessed to be around 600 years. By 1932, when it was cut down, its trunk was hollow and could accommodate 31 adults.

Grace Dewes, a descendent of one of Glenview's founding families, began her teaching career at age 16 in a one-room school. Her collection of historic books and photographs are a valuable part of the historical society's collection.

In rural America, one-room schoolhouses were the norm. One teacher taught all eight grades. Pupils sat in one room and listened as others recited their lessons. Boys often attended only during the winter months, because they were needed to help out on the farm during spring planting and fall harvest.

The first Rugen School was built in 1902 on Telegraph Road (now Shermer Avenue) just north of present-day Lake Avenue. Initially a one-room schoolhouse, a second room was added in 1915. By 1941, there were four rooms with six teachers. When the Glenview Naval Air Station expanded at the beginning of World War II, the school was demolished. The site is now part of Glenview's public works campus.

The same year the Immanuel Lutheran Church was built (1876), a school was founded as a Christian day school. By 1922, there were 80 students in the newly expanded two-room schoolhouse.

When the Glenview School was built in 1905, it provided village children with a spacious learning environment—a far cry from the old one-room schools. In the early part of the 20th century, it was not unusual for students to end their education after grade 8. Glenview kids who wished to go on to high school usually traveled to New Trier or commuted by train to Carl Schurz in Chicago. There was a short-lived attempt to establish a high school program within Glenview School during the 1920s; it lasted but three years. The building's final reuse was that of District 34's administration building until it was razed in the early 1970s to make way for a new village hall.

Baseball was one of the country's most popular pastimes at the beginning of the 20th century. This 1903 team played on a field located on the northwest side of Waukegan Road and Lake Street (now Glenview Road). By the 1920s, semiprofessional teams were to be found throughout the suburbs, and Glenview's own was outstanding. The ballpark moved to a triangular-shaped piece of land between River Road and Dewes Street west of Waukegan Road. Surrounded by a high board fence, the field included bleachers for spectators and a large wooden scoreboard. When no games were scheduled, military bands from Great Lakes and Fort Sheridan sometimes gave performances at the park.

The first volunteer fire company was organized on December 6, 1911. By September 1912, there were 25 volunteers, and a secondhand fire engine was purchased for their use. In 1937, a rural fire association was formed to protect homeowners outside village limits. A modern stone firehouse was built for the still-volunteer company on Glenview Road at Pine Street in 1948. The department became a full-time professional organization in 1960.

One of the many nursery businesses in the village was that of Charles Palmgren. Established in 1909, it was redeveloped into the Carriage Hill townhome complex in 1959.

The old wooden Grove Street bridge was replaced by a more substantial bridge in 1916. In the late 1800s and early 1900s, the river was a major source of fun for residents, with activities such as ice-skating, swimming, and fishing. At one time, the river was 60 feet wide and only 3 to 4 feet deep. Dredging deepened the channel in 1926.

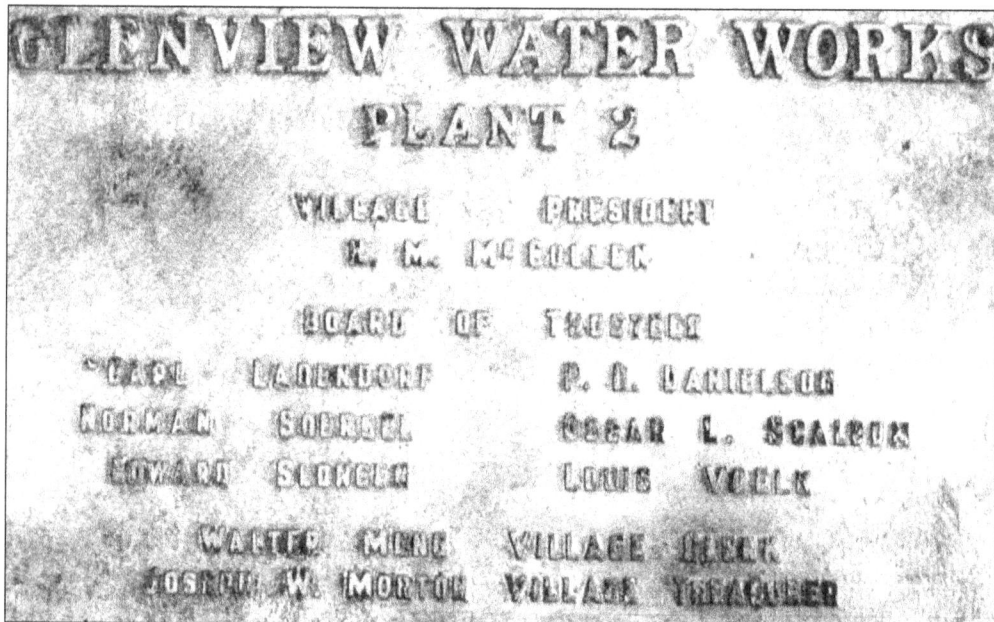

Several flowing wells in the area, powered by hand pumps and windmills, were the initial sources of water in early Glenview. The first municipal deep well was dug in 1916, with a village-wide water system in place in 1917. A sewer system was built five years later. By 1925, a second waterworks plant was necessary to meet public demand. Wells continued to provide the municipal water supply until 1946 (some sources indicate 1938), when the village contracted with Wilmette for Lake Michigan water.

42

Glenview's nearly unlimited supply of clay provided raw material for making brick and tile. Lutter Brick Company opened in Glenview in 1905. Occupying a 150-acre site north of the railroad off West Lake (now Chestnut) Avenue, it was one of the largest brickyards in the Chicago area. The old Lutter family home remains an imposing residence at Glenview and Drake Roads.

John Rugen ran the Lutter Brick Company's steam engine, which hauled clay from the pit to the production plant. After the business was discontinued, the pit became the village's trash dump.

The *c.* 1910 wedding of Mathilda Rugen and Henry Lutter united two of Glen View's prominent families. Henry was village president from 1935 to 1941.

Edwin S. Jackman made his fortune as the Chicago
agent for Firth-Sterling Steel Company. A resident
of the neighboring village of Golf, he was a
philanthropist whose generosity benefited Glen View
through the donation of the bear fountain, which
ultimately came to be the village's trademark. Jackman
later donated a second fountain, *The Spirit of Youth*, to
the Glen View Golf and Polo Club.

1917

The entire village turned out for the dedication of the bear fountain in 1917. Music was
furnished by a band from Great Lakes Naval Training Center. Everyone from village dignitaries
to schoolchildren took part in the huge celebration. The fountain's original location was on
Lake Street (now Glenview Road) near the current downtown firehouse.

Following the dedication of the bear fountain in 1917, the village instituted an annual celebration of the event in 1918. Called Fountain Day, the celebration evolved into Glenview Days a few years later. For many years, the event was held on Prairie Street between Washington and Depot Streets. Festivities included water fights between fire companies, tumbling clowns, tricycle parades for boys, doll parades for girls, a Mardi Gras–like costume parade, street dances, and baseball games.

A whimsical illustration graced the cover of the bear foundation program at its dedication. Images of animals, birds, reptiles, and Native Americans were carved on the pedestal that supported the bear statue. The fountain was designed to supply a refreshing drink of water at three different levels—for people, horses, and pets.

Among the many young men to serve in World War I was C. D. Rugen's son Fred.

Joseph M. Sesterhenn was just 17 when he enlisted in the army during World War I. His parents, Michael and Clara, had five children; Joseph was their only son. Serving in Company M, 18th Infantry, he was critically wounded in the Battle of the Argonne on October 4, 1918, and died the same day. Of the 70 young men from Glen View to serve in World War I, he was the only fatality. Glenview's American Legion Post 166 was named in his honor.

Honor Roll

BOYS FROM DISTRICT OF
Glenview, Illinois

Who have answered the Call of their Country

Carl Anderson
Jessie Anderson
Arthur Barnitz
Raymond Bartling
Godfrie Blackman
Rudolph Beherndt
Nicholas Biederer
Samuel Hubert
Arthur Burnham
Crebert Barnham
Lawrence Burnham
George Butzow
Elmer Clavey
Charles Cole

John W. Dewes
William Dewes
Edwin Eberstien
William Eberstien
Erwin Eggert
George Eggestien
William Eggestien
Joe Fagen
George Frake
Arthur Gardner
Fred Geffe
John Gizmer
Alvin Gyllenhaal
William Hagen

William Hagen
Edward Hattendorf
George Hattendorf
Fred Homan
Gustave Homan
Herman Johnas
Carl Johnson
Felix Jange
Arthur King
John Kasseldt
Robert Landwehr
George Long
William Long
William Long

George Lorentz
William Lorenz
Ben McQueen
Harold McQueen
Lester McKinzie
Norman Melzer
Hans Miersch
Lawrence Myrkle
Fred Raddatz
Herbert Rugen
Walter Rugen
John Russet
George Schippman
Fred Schnadt

★ Joe Sesterhenn
Frank Stander
Walter Sternberg
Allen Synestvedt
Ralph Synestvedt
Henry Tatge
Rudolph Tagtmeier
Albert Teskie
Fred Triebold
Louie Triebold
Harry Werhan
Vine Westbrook
Henry Wille
Fred Vollman

This World War I honor roll is on display in the Farmhouse Museum of the Glenview Area Historical Society. Nearly every family name in Glenview's early history is represented.

Three

ENTREPRENEURS, ONIONS, AND THE MOB

In the years following World War I, the nation enjoyed a robust economy that fueled a building boom. Homes, businesses, golf courses, and polo fields sprang up in the village, creating an image of Glen View as a rich man's playground. The Prohibition act of 1920 spawned expansion of organized crime, including bootleg liquor, gambling, and prostitution, throughout the United States. Mob activity was rampant in Chicago and its suburbs, and Glen View did not escape. There were two airfields—Curtiss-Reynolds and Northwest (the latter located in the triangle between Milwaukee Avenue and Central and Greenwood Roads). The Curtiss-Reynolds-Wright Airport included schools for pilots and mechanics; elaborate plans were in the works for a fly-in country club, which would include the Pickwick Golf Club. The stock market crash of October 29, 1929, brought to a halt the grand dreams of many businessmen. The excesses of the Roaring Twenties were followed by the deprivations of the 1930s. Plans were scuttled for a horse-racing track on the site that ultimately became home to the Convent of the Holy Spirit. The Glenview Symphony and Northfield Civic Chorus were formed; their concerts provided welcome low-cost entertainment. Meanwhile, agriculture continued to sustain Glenview's economy, just as it had for the past 100 years. But now the farms were smaller truck farms, and crops were mostly flowers and vegetables. Farmers hired local youths and adults to pick onions for 20¢ per bushel. The village's chamber of commerce promoted Glenview as a "village of homes and gardens."

Many roadhouses were to be found in the unincorporated areas surrounding Glenview. In 1913, one of these, the House That Jack Built, was located near where Milwaukee Avenue crosses the Des Plaines River south of Willow Road. Like most such businesses, it had a reputation as a gin joint during Prohibition. By 1960, the property had been completely renovated and opened as the elegant Villa Venice Supper Club; Chicago mobster Sam Giancana was a silent owner. Gondolas plied the waters of the adjacent Des Plaines River, and ladies of the evening were available to those who wished feminine company. Frank Sinatra and the Rat Pack headlined a show at the Villa Venice in November 1962. Eddie Fisher opened for the main attraction, which included Sammy Davis Jr. and Dean Martin. A fire destroyed the nightclub in March 1967; a hotel and restaurant complex occupies the site today.

In post–World War I Glenview, the downtown was growing. Some former homes had been converted to stores; these were interspersed with new brick buildings along Glenview Road. In the foreground, at the corner of Church Street and Glenview Road, is the building that housed the Noffz Drug Store and the post office around 1920. Today the appearance of the exterior is largely unchanged.

51

After John Dilg purchased Al Eustis's tavern in 1899, he added a third floor. Known as Dilg's Tavern or the Glen View House, the building became a social and civic center and variously housed church services, dances, and classrooms in the upper-story rooms when the schools became overcrowded.

Glenview State Bank opened for business in May 1921 with capital of $30,000. This bank replaced a small one that operated from the Rugen Brothers Stores and was established a few years earlier by a group of citizens. Glenview State Bank was robbed on September 24, 1921, resulting in the death of the cashier, Fred J. Christenson. The bank experienced a number of close calls with gangsters over the years, but there were no further fatalities.

The "modern" Rugen Stores building came on the scene in 1905. A kind of early mini-mall, it housed grocery, hardware, clothing, and dry goods stores under one roof.

When Glenview's first athletic club outgrew the space in August Clavey's workshop, C. D. Rugen built a two-story structure behind Rugen Stores. The second floor was given over to an athletic club. C. D.'s sons belonged, as did most of the able-bodied men in the village. In addition to boxing and wrestling, there was space for basketball and indoor baseball.

This view of the grocery section of Rugen's vividly demonstrates that canned foods were abundant in the 1920s. Although refrigeration was already a reality, frozen products would not become widely available until after World War II.

The Blue Heron restaurant was famous for its chicken dinners. Folks from Chicago's North Side often called in a dinner order, and it would be ready when they arrived in Glen View. When Glenview Road was extended to link up with the east side of the village about 1926, one wing of the building was moved across the street to house a bakery.

When G. H. Jacobsen initiated development of Glen Oak Acres in the mid-1920s, his advertising promoted its idyllic wooded setting. He noted an added attraction as the close proximity to seven established golf courses, a major interest of the day. Soon after this advertising was launched, an eighth course, Pickwick, opened about a mile and a half to the west of the subdivision.

The Road to Happiness Lies Through Glen Oak Acres

⌐if You Are a Golfer

For the golfer and to insure the perpetual majesty of your home, pause and think of these surroundings—

Sunset Ridge Country Club . . . . . ½ mile north
North Shore Golf Club . . . . .1300 feet south
Wilmette Golf Club . . . . .1300 feet east
Glen View Golf Club . . . . .1 mile south
Glen Acres . . . . .1 mile southwest
Indian Hill Country Club . . . . . .1½ miles northeast
Westmoreland Country Club . . . .2 miles southeast

Name if you can another location possessing surroundings to compare with Glen Oak Acres.

G. H. JACOBSEN,

Phone Glenview 80   Glenview, Ill.

The Joseph Zander home on Pleasant Lane was the second house built in Glen Oak Acres. This back view of the home and yard is indicative of the size and setting of the homes planned for that development. (Courtesy of the Zander collection.)

It required six years and a concerted effort by Glenview citizens to raise money for a civic building. The impressive structure was dedicated on September 7, 1929. The facility housed not only government offices and public meeting rooms but also the first public library in its west wing. Glenview's first public park surrounded the building. The World War I–era cannon mounted in front of the building was likely given over to a scrap metal drive during World War II. When a new village hall was finished in 1974, the old civic building became headquarters for the park district's administration offices and became a local landmark.

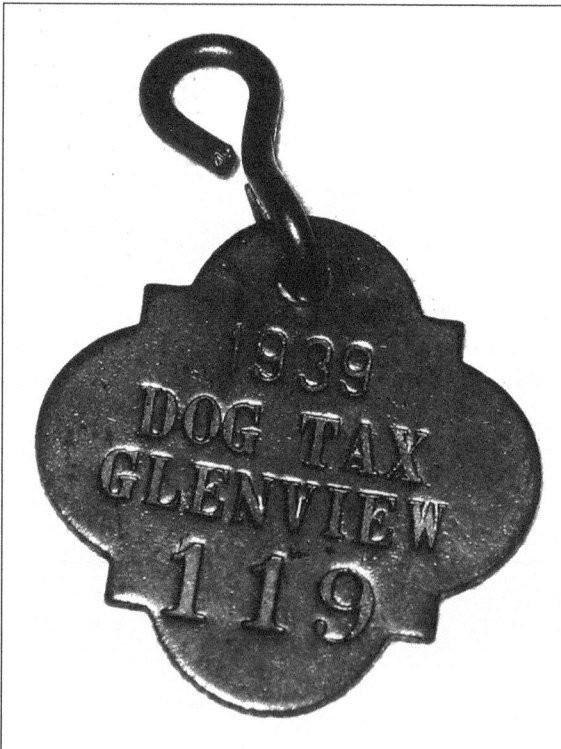

Vehicle licenses were first required in 1919; traffic ordinances followed two years later. Within 20 years, residents were required to license their dogs as well.

By the late 1930s, the look of Glenview's downtown had changed a bit as the North Shore Dairy joined two grocery stores—the A&P and the Royal Blue store.

Scalbom Machine Tool Company was located on Glenview Road between Washington Street and Lehigh Avenue. The Scalboms moved their business from Chicago to Glenview in 1921. The building was full of lathes, drill presses, and other machines for building or repairing just about anything with moving parts. When the public library next door expanded in the late 1960s, the building was demolished to make way for parking.

The old police station was located next to the firehouse on Pine Street. Before the village police initiated a radio system in 1938, a light atop the village water tower alerted an officer to a call. He would contact the telephone operator, who would then pass the message along.

George Kilroy was Glenview's first rookie motorcycle policeman in 1930. His salary was $30 per month, and he had to furnish his own motorcycle. The depressed economic times were reflected in the fact that the town marshal's pay in 1917 had been $40 per month. Kilroy retired as police chief in 1951.

Around 1938, developer George F. Nixon began work on a planned community that required homes to be built with interrelation and conformity to their own minimum half-acre sites. Selling prices ranged from $16,000 to $25,000; targeted buyers' annual incomes were between $5,000 and $12,000. The first five homes built were sold—in spite of the fact the country was just emerging from the Great Depression. The development was called Glen Ayre and is still a prestigious neighborhood within the village. Here Nixon's wife, Elsie, is pictured in the garden of the family home in Glen Ayre. About a decade earlier, Nixon had planned to build a Chicago Gold Coast–type complex in Glen Ayre. Designed to appeal to wealthy Chicagoans who could commute to Glenview via the Chicago North Shore and Milwaukee Railroad (which had a station on Glenview Road just west of today's Edens Expressway), the plan called for an elaborate complex of sumptuous condominium-type residences. Every amenity—from shopping to medical care to athletic facilities—was to be included within the complex. The Depression, however, put an end to that grand plan.

In the 1920s, the Glenview Dramatics Club provided lively public performances. This one, titled *The Spinster's Club Had Gone to Smash*, was directed by Clement McCarthy, a Miss Dulmadge, and Mrs. C. D. Rugen.

Mabel Rugen, a daughter of C. D. Rugen, was determined to get an education. Many parents of the day were not in favor of sending their daughters to college, but Mabel was able to persuade her father. She earned an undergraduate degree at the University of Wisconsin and a doctorate at New York University. She was a professor of public health at the University of Michigan for 40 years and earned many honors during that time. Her cousin Myrtle Rugen was an outstanding educator and administrator in Glenview schools for 32 years.

In an effort to provide a safe route for students to cross busy Waukegan Road to the Glenview School, a tunnel was dug under the street in the mid-1920s.

Chicago's WBBM radio station, a CBS affiliate, began broadcasting in October 1927. Its broadcast tower was erected near Telegraph (now Shermer) Avenue, south of Willow Road, and was originally owned by the Atlas Investment Company. There seemed little concern about the potential hazard when the Curtiss-Reynolds Airfield was constructed on adjacent land two years later.

As a young man, Joseph Roseman played an excellent game of golf. He turned out to be a talented designer of golf courses as well. His invention of the gang mower for cutting golf course greens resulted in the establishment of the Roseman Tractor Company, first located in Evanston and later in Glenview.

Roseman's 36-hole Pickwick Golf Club opened in 1927. A plan for an elegant clubhouse was a victim of the stock market crash two years later. The golf course was part of the property purchased by the navy and was reduced to 18 holes when runways were expanded in 1942. After Naval Air Station Glenview closed in 1995, the park district operated the course for a few years as the Station Links. Currently a series of townhomes occupy the site.

The
Garden of Allah
Waukegan Road
at Glenview, Ill.

One of Glen View's most elegant restaurants was the Garden of Allah, located on the land where the Lyon School now stands. Decorated with red velvet drapes and upholstery, it was rumored to have been run by the organized crime syndicate. Old-timers told of its abrupt closure in the 1920s following the discovery of a woman's body on the patio of the establishment.

Ted Borre moved his barbershop from Dilg's Tavern to this location on Glenview Road just west of the railroad tracks about 1928. The business also housed a small beauty salon. The building was ultimately demolished to make way for a dry cleaning shop.

GRAND CONCERT

Given By

Northfield Township Civic Chorus

and

Glenview Civic Orchestra

SUNDAY AFTERNOON, FEBRUARY 19, 1933

Catholic Hall — Glenview, Illinois

3:30 o'clock   154   Adults 50c

Although times were hard during the Depression, culture was abundant in the village. The Glenview Music Foundation sponsored the Northfield Civic Chorus and Glenview Civic Orchestra, which offered three or four performances each season. The foundation's motto was "good music takes a place among the finer things."

One of the village's best-known music men was Jesse Stevens, who taught in Glenview for 60 years. In addition to tutoring countless Glenview children, he conducted the civic orchestra and chorus. His work extended into Chicago as well; he was founder of the Logan Square Conservatory of Music.

The old River Inn was located on Wagner Road, north of Lake Avenue. It was later renamed Willow on Wagner. Tales of 1930s mob activity at the restaurant and bar flourished until it was demolished some 70 years later. One of its most famous "alums" was said to be George "Baby Face" Nelson.

The venerable Meier's Tavern looks very much the same today as it did when it opened in 1935. It replaced a barn which operated as a speakeasy in the 1920s.

In 1935, Link's Homestead at Waukegan Road and Lake Avenue advertised "good food and good entertainment." Link's Bavarians provided lively musical entertainment.

Phone Glenview 195   We Cater to Parties

VILLA DEL MAR

— *Barbeque* —

CHICKEN DINNERS — PLATE LUNCHES

Where people who enjoy a good
dinner find the highest degree
of satisfaction.

Northeast Corner Waukegan Rd. and Lake Ave.

GLENVIEW   ILLINOIS

Villa Del Mar, with its Spanish-style architecture, was opened by John Adinamis on the northeast corner of Waukegan Road and Lake Avenue in 1929, six months before the stock market crash. The restaurant and adjacent gasoline station survived the Depression and became Reynaldo's Piano Lounge in 1951. About 20 years later, it burned to the ground. Today the site is part of Glen Oak Plaza.

Glenview's other bear—Tootsie—found her way to Glenview in an unusual way. Glenview contractor Joe Zander and Fr. Joseph Fitzgerald, assistant pastor at Our Lady of Perpetual Help, encountered Tootsie while on a fishing trip to Canada in 1938. Apparently an orphan, the cub attached itself to the two gentlemen. Not wishing to leave the cub to fend for itself in the wilderness, they decided to bring it back to Glenview. After a series of negotiations with officials at the Canadian border, Tootsie came to live with the Zander family. Sitting upright, balanced on her hindquarters, Tootsie enjoys a bottle of Coca-Cola at the Zander Standard Oil station located at Waukegan and Henley Streets. Bill White, station manager, looks on. (Courtesy of the Zander collection.)

Quality Products

Served

COURTEOUSLY
EFFICIENTLY
and
INTELLIGENTLY

—

THE PURE OIL STATION

in
GLENVIEW

Glenview & Waukegan Rds.

A familiar sight on Waukegan Road at River Drive is the former Pure Oil station. The building's exterior remains very similar to its look in the 1930s.

After having an itinerant existence for nearly a century, Glenview's own post office was finally welcomed on Lehigh Avenue. By the time the new facility opened in 1930, the village's name had evolved into one word—Glenview. The post office remained at this location for about 24 years.

69

Baxter Laboratories opened its first manufacturing plant in Glenview in 1933. An automobile showroom, located on Waukegan Road at the river, was remodeled to accommodate equipment necessary to manufacture a total of five types of intravenous solutions. In the beginning, there were six employees.

BAXTER LABORATORIES, INC.

GLENVIEW, ILLINOIS	**COLLEGE POINT, N. Y.**
TORONTO, CANADA	**LONDON, ENGLAND**

———●———

Manufacturers of

BAXTER'S INTRAVENOUS SOLUTIONS

IN VACOLITERS AND BLOOD TRANSFUSION

EQUIPMENT

By 1939, the company had developed a sterile vacuum-type system for the collection and storage of blood. During World War II, production at the plant increased dramatically as medical supplies destined for the military were shipped from Glenview to the far corners of the globe.

FOR SPORT
— and —
RECREATION
— at —
GLENVIEW'S 12
MODERN ALLEYS

League Season Opening Date
September 15th, 1938

Glenview Recreation Co.
630 Waukegan Road
Telephones Glenview 678 and 778

From its beginning in 1927, the Glenview Bowl was a center of entertainment for adults and children alike. Owner Ed Bruhn was a good baseball player. In his younger years, he was a pitcher for the old St. Louis Browns farm club.

One room of the bowling alley housed a bar and pool tables, making it a favorite evening out for adults. After being a fixture on Waukegan Road for more than 50 years, it was destroyed by fire. The property is now the site of an automobile dealership.

One of the oldest restaurants still operating in Glenview is Matty's Wayside Inn, originally a farmhouse built in 1890. Matty Sr. and Erna Fegers bought the property in 1931 and opened a small restaurant toward the end of Prohibition. It was one of the area's many "blind pigs," or eateries which also served illegal liquor. The building was remodeled in 1941 and again in 1957, when the enclosed porch still in use today was added.

One part of Pres. Franklin D. Roosevelt's New Deal during the 1930s was the Civilian Conservation Corps (CCC). The program, which began in 1933 and ended in 1942, was designed to provide work for the unemployed. The mission of the young men stationed at Camp Skokie (also called Camp Glenview) was to dig the Skokie Lagoons to drain the swampy land in the region. The complex was located in the forest preserve at Harms Road and Lake Avenue.

Glenview resident Charles Rieb received a discharge from the CCC program in 1934.

The CCC was run in military style, with barracks, uniforms, and officers in charge. The training proved extremely useful, as many of the former CCC boys went into the armed services when the United States entered World War II.

MESS HALL

The program was a godsend for the approximately two million young men who participated. It provided three meals a day, a place to sleep, and medical and dental care, as well as a chance to learn a trade. The CCC program ended about the time World War II began, and Camp Skokie was given over to the army to house a military police facility.

The words *Hackney's* and *hamburgers* are still synonymous in Glenview. Hackney's first restaurant and bar was established in 1939 on Harms Road. Located across from the military police installation in the forest preserve, personnel managed to have the pub declared part of the camp so that they might visit without leaving the post. When the post became a prisoner of war camp about 1943, the German prisoners incarcerated there debated with their army guards the virtues of American versus German beer. The Germans said they would need to taste the American version to know which was best. It was reported that the Americans never took them up on the proposal.

The 130-acre Appleyard farm on Telegraph Road (now Shermer Avenue) was redeveloped as the Glen Acres Golf Club in 1924. The 100-year-old Appleyard barn was converted into a clubhouse, which survived until 1964. Joseph Roseman operated the facility and renamed it Elmgate in 1930. It was renamed again in 1946 and was known as the Chesterfield Golf Club. The Glenview Park District bought the property in 1955, operating it as a public golf course.

Glenview's chamber of commerce evolved from its predecessor, the Glenview Civic Association, about 1930. The chamber sponsored its first golf tournament at Elmgate in 1932.

John and Katharina Wagner emigrated from Germany to what became South Northfield in 1837. They homesteaded a farm of more than 100 acres and raised nine children. One of their sons, Thomas, married Julia Brachtendorf and raised five children on the farm. Three of them, Peter, Lucy, and Rose, never married and worked together to keep the farm going. They maintained a small herd of Holstein cows, which was an unusual sight in a suburban area. Peter kept an American flag hanging from the barn's hayloft window as a navigation aid to the pilots flying into Naval Air Station Glenview. Rose was the last survivor of the family, and after her death in the late 1990s, the farm was purchased by the Glenview Park District. Today it is operated as the Historic Wagner Farm and Heritage Center.

Although Chicago's municipal airport had served the city's commercial aviation interests since 1927, visibility in the skies above Chicago was compromised by smog. Seeking relief from those conditions, the Curtiss Flying Service contracted to build a major airport away from the city. Curtiss and the Wright Aeronautical Corporation merged about the time the airfield was completed. Called Curtiss-Reynolds, Curtiss-Wright, or Curtiss Chicago, the field was dedicated on October 20, 1929. The stock market crashed nine days later, and the airport struggled along during the Depression. It was customary to paint the name of the airfield on the roof of a hangar in the days before radio navigation.

National air races, usually held in Cleveland, were scheduled at Curtiss in 1930. Thousands of spectators converged upon Glenview, causing traffic jams on the few roads leading to the village.

Art Chester, a prominent designer of racing airplanes and a pilot himself, lived in Glenview during the 1930s. His most famous design was named the Jeep, after a cartoon of the day.

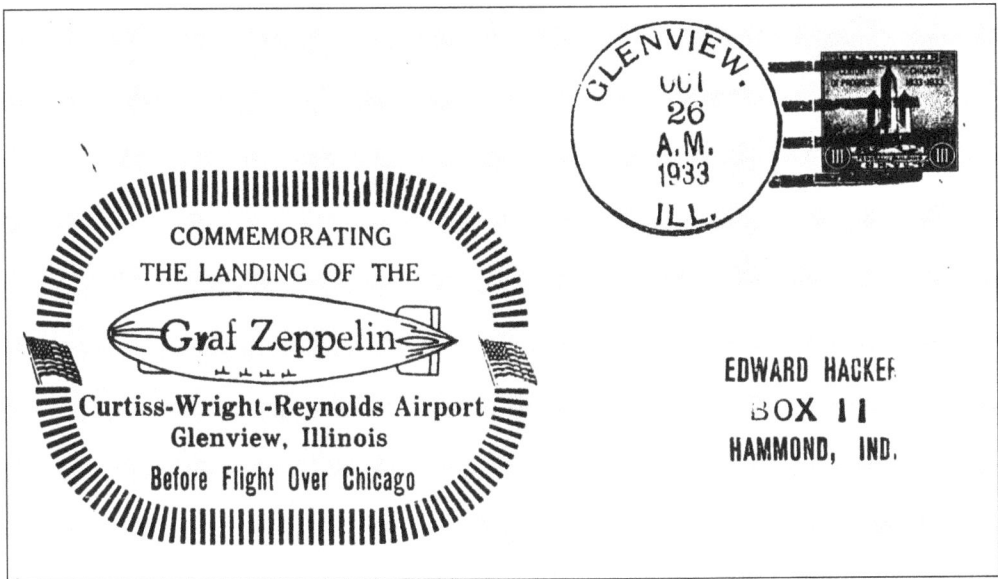

The *Graf Zeppelin* dirigible was one of the most famous airships of the day. The mammoth cigar-shaped aircraft was scheduled to fly over Chicago's Century of Progress International Exposition (world's fair) on October 26, 1933. The much-anticipated event was to include a stop at Glenview's Curtiss Airport. Dozens of men were in place on the ground to handle the lines as the dirigible arrived. Deteriorating weather forced a change of plans, and the ship landed for only about 20 minutes—just time enough to off-load some passengers and mail. The big airship headed for its home base in Akron, Ohio, forcing cancellation of a planned stop in Milwaukee.

Women pilots were part of the air race scene almost from the beginning. Florence Klingensmith was young, beautiful, and a fearless competitor. At the 1930 air races, she flew a Gee Bee racing plane that had been modified. The engine was too powerful for the airframe, and the fabric on the wings disintegrated. Spectators reported that she steered the plane away from the crowds and crashed in the Swain Nelson property southeast of the field. The accident took her life; she was 23.

In 1936, the Chicago Girls Flying Club, the National Women Pilots Association, and the Ninety-Nines cosponsored Rod-Air-O at Curtiss. Headquarters for the event, which was broadcast nationally via NBC Radio, was at the Medinah Temple in Chicago.

ROD-AIR-O

ALL
GIRL FLYERS
CURTISS AIRPORT
GLENVIEW, ILL.

When Naval Reserve Aviation Base Chicago was dedicated on August 28, 1937, Glenview dignitaries attended, along with distinguished military guests. The chamber of commerce joined in the celebration by issuing a commemorative stamp.

The navy leased the north three-fifths of the Curtiss hangar to serve as headquarters for Naval Reserve Aviation Base Chicago. Both navy and civilian aviation facilities coexisted in the hangar until the beginning of World War II. The space was remodeled and expanded several times.

NEW AIR SERVICE FOR NORTH SHORE

New air schedules, effective April 1, from the North Shore to New York, Cleveland, Washington and other principal cities reduces air travel time to the east considerably. United Air Lines will operate the service, which provides for departure from the Curtis Airport in Glenview at 8:25 a.m. connecting with eastb[...] Mainliners at the Chicago Municipal Airport. G[...] twin-engined, three-mile-a-minute Boeing transp[...] similar to the one shown above, will be used on the t[...] ty-mile flight from Glenview to the Chicago Air[...]

On April 1, 1938, United Airlines initiated flights from the Curtiss Airport to Municipal (now Midway) Airport. Maj. R. W. Schroeder, who had overseen construction of Curtiss and was now a United Airlines vice president, announced that Boeing twin-engine Mainliners would leave Curtiss beginning at 8:45 a.m. to reach the Chicago field 20 minutes later. Passengers could then connect to flights to New York, Washington, D.C., Cleveland, and other principal eastern cities. There were eight flights per day from Curtiss between the hours of 10:00 a.m. and 5:00 p.m. Called the "North Shore Special," these flights were advertised as decreasing the previous flying time for North Shore passengers by one hour.

Swain Nelson, a Swedish immigrant, initially established the Nelson and Sons Landscape Company in Chicago. Extremely successful, the company soon grew to include a London office. Among the many projects that added to its fame and fortune was the landscaping of Chicago's Lincoln Park and the 1893 World's Columbian Exposition (world's fair). As a part of the Swedenborg Society in Chicago, the Nelson family decided to relocate to Oak Glen. They purchased 60 acres from Joseph Kinder between present-day Elm Street and Shermer Road in 1892. Swain, along with sons Seymour and Alvin, planted nursery stock on the former farmland to expand his thriving business.

328 ACRE TESTING LABORATORY

328 acres of the finest shrubs and trees comprise Swain Nelson & Sons Co. testing laboratory for tree care. Here not only tree spraying, but also tree trimming, tree feeding, and tree surgery have reached the highest scientific development. More than 80 years of experience in landscape gardening and tree care makes Swain Nelson & Sons Co. acknowledged leaders in this important work.

Office of Swain Nelson & Sons Co. at Glenview, Illinois

SWAIN NELSON AND SONS CO., GLENVIEW, ILLINOIS

The Swain Nelson Landscape Company eventually grew to 328 acres and included the land upon which now stands the Swainwood and Tall Trees neighborhoods. The lush look of those areas is due, in part, to many trees and shrubs originally planted by the firm.

The Swain Nelson Landscape Company headquarters building has changed little since it housed the company's offices. Located near the entrance to Roosevelt Park on Glenview Road, it now houses the United Way, Glenview Chamber of Commerce, Glenview Art League, and other offices.

A large fleet of trucks and heavy equipment was necessary to support the business.

The Haut Funeral Home opened in 1936 and served the village for many years. The building still stands on Waukegan Road and now houses stores and offices.

ALFRED J. HAUT'S FUNERAL HOME
1114 Waukegan Road   Telephone Glenview 83   Glenview
Sixteen years rendering a dignified conscientious service.
AMBULANCE SERVICE DAY AND NIGHT

In 1932, land was purchased to develop a large park for the village. A government grant and labor provided by the Works Progress Administration got the program rolling. Named Roosevelt Park, there was space for a swimming pool, tennis courts, a baseball diamond, and a children's playground. The public turned out to celebrate its dedication in 1935.

Carl Ladendorf's market was located at the corner of Lehigh and Glenview Roads. Several posters are visible among displays in the windows. These let customers know this store was in compliance with the National Recovery Administration laws enacted in 1933 to set codes for competitive fair pricing during the Depression. The laws were declared unconstitutional two years later.

Roosevelt Park Field House has served many functions, including providing locker room space for the swimming pool and space for public meetings. In 1933, John "Jake the Barber" Factor was held captive, ostensibly by the Touhy gang, in a house not far from here while the park was under construction.

The big round swimming pool was finally finished in 1940. When original funding fell short, the Glenview Days committee raised $5,000 to complete the project. Much to the delight of the village's children, Roosevelt Park Pool was a reality at last.

George and William Keck were among the foremost American architects of solar homes. Their contemporary designs included flat roofs, radiant heating, indirect lighting, and passive solar heating. About 1940, the Keck brothers and Todd Sloan built a series of homes in the Solar Park subdivision. The streets in the subdivision included Redwood, Solar, and Edgewood Lanes. Additional solar homes were built in other locations nearby. Many of these Keck houses in Glenview have been demolished.

Four

WARTIME AND BEYOND

The bombing of Pearl Harbor triggered a declaration of war by the United States, first against Japan, then against Germany. Record numbers of Glenview's young men enlisted in the armed forces, while many young women from the village entered the women's branches of the military services. Within the space of a few months, Naval Reserve Aviation Base Chicago expanded into a training facility for primary, and later for carrier, pilots. Folks on the home front prepared for the worst and formed civil defense units in anticipation of bombing raids and possible invasion by Japanese and German forces. As the war progressed, the old CCC camp at Harms Road and Lake Avenue was refurbished to become a military police facility, then a prisoner of war camp. Businesses refocused toward manufacturing products for the war effort. The Swain Nelson Landscape Company turned its facilities into a factory to produce optics, including components for bomb sights. Baxter Laboratories stepped up production of intravenous fluids and blood plasma for the military's medical corps. Everyone who was able—men who did not qualify for military service, teenagers, housewives, even senior citizens—had no trouble finding employment. As Glenview and the entire nation moved into the mode of producing materials for the war effort, economic recovery became a reality. The 1940 census pegged the population of Glenview at 2,500; the village surely contributed as much per capita to the war effort as any municipality in the country. As veterans began to return to Glenview after the war ended in 1945, another building boom was underway and the population soared.

The Glenview Days celebration in the summer of 1941 was the last prewar festival. The celebrations continued during World War II, but the theme changed to reflect a nation at war.

In the early 1940s, stores on Glenview's main street (Glenview Road) included Leverniers' Grocery and Renneckar's Drug Store, along with stores located within converted residences.

One of the last buildings to be completed before World War II did away with building materials for civilian construction was a modern dental office located on Pine Street just north of Glenview Road. This advertisement, which appeared in the 1942 Glenview Days program, demonstrates that its original appearance is not very different from that of today. The building was renovated into a residence about 2005.

. . . . to visit Glenview's new Medical and Dental Building. Nurses in attendance will be glad to show you through at any time.

●

THEODORE H. KRUMM, M. D.

JOSEPH A. BOBROW, D. D. S.

●

Prairie Avenue and Pine Street (One block east of C. M. & St. P. depot, Glenview)

Glenview is the Home of—

"The Personality Home of 1942"

One of Our Lady of Perpetual Help's most dynamic priests was Fr. John Dussman. During the Depression, the parish incurred a sizeable debt. Among Dussman's ideas for fund-raising to help retire the debt was construction and sale of "personality homes." Parishioners donated material and labor for the project. The first efforts involved rehabilitating existing homes. Later new homes were constructed and raffled off. The raffles were extremely popular with Chicago residents, as well as those living in the suburbs. Pictured is the personality home of 1942.

Drama clubs helped keep spirits up during the war years. The Glenview Players' 1942 production, *Holiday*, drew upon local talent, including Kenneth and Anita Ramsay, who later were founding members of the Glenview Area Historical Society.

GLENVIEW PLAYERS

PRESENT...

Holiday

FRIDAY & SATURDAY
NOV. 19-20

GLENVIEW SCHOOL
AUDITORIUM

ALL STAR LOCAL CAST

Admission..... $1.00
Tax 10
$1.10

Following the attack on Pearl Harbor on December 7, 1941, the pace at Naval Reserve Aviation Base Chicago accelerated immediately. In 1942, the base expanded into a small city within 121 working days.

By the time expansion was complete, there were paved runways for both primary trainers and the larger aircraft used for the carrier qualification training program. The circular pads were used by the little biplane trainers. This aerial shows not only the base itself but also a great deal of undeveloped land surrounding the military installation.

Naval Reserve Aviation Base Chicago shifted gears rapidly at the beginning of World War II. The base's location in the center of the country deemed it somewhat less vulnerable to enemy attack than installations closer to both coasts.

Small yellow biplanes—Stearmans or N3Ns—were used for primary training. The biplanes were nicknamed "yellow perils," a moniker that aptly described the uncertainties of the early phases of pilot training. Glenview was the largest primary training base in the country and was designated Naval Air Station Glenview in 1943.

Hangar One became the nerve center of operations for primary training and later for the carrier qualification training unit.

Nearly every carrier pilot who qualified during World War II did so at Naval Air Station Glenview. The program used two makeshift carriers, the USS *Sable* and the USS *Wolverine*; both were converted Lake Michigan excursion side-wheelers. Here a plane takes off from the deck of the USS *Sable*.

Although not a naval aviator, Lt. Comdr. Gerald Ford served aboard the aircraft carrier USS *Monterey* in the South Pacific. After the war, he was stationed at Naval Air Station Glenview, where he was staff physical and military training officer, during his final six months of service.

George Herbert Walker Bush was just 19 years old when he successfully completed carrier qualification training at Glenview. He was the second-youngest World War II naval aviator. It is likely that few military bases can boast two future presidents (Ford and Bush) among its alumni. (Courtesy of the Bush Library collection.)

Matinee idol Robert Taylor's career took him from Hollywood during the 1930s to Glenview for his role as a navy flight instructor during the war. His prewar flying experience served the nation well. Among his duties was to make training films for aviation cadets.

WAR DEPARTMENT
THE ADJUTANT GENERAL'S OFFICE
WASHINGTON, D. C.

OFFICIAL BUSINESS

CHICAGO
MAY 14
9:30 PM
1942

PENALTY FOR PRIVATE USE TO AVOID
PAYMENT OF POSTAGE, $300

BUY
DEFENSE SAVINGS
BONDS AND STAMPS

August Rugen
Shermer Avenue,
Glenview, Illinois.

When the naval air station expanded early in 1942, the August Rugen home was condemned, and the family was required to move on very short notice. The war impacted the family in another way as well when Rugen's sons were drafted into military service. This postcard notifies the family that Raymond, having passed his physical, is on his way to basic training.

During World War II, many families of German origin shared the same dilemma as the Rugens—there were family members in both American and German armies. Not unlike the mixed emotions of the Civil War, families often awaited news of relatives on both sides. Rugen nephew Harry Rodel writes to his aunt and uncle from an Allied prisoner of war camp in France.

19. Mai 45. Unteroffizier Harry Roedel,
31G-517989-GERMAN-8426 Labor Service Co.(9)
PWIB-France.
Liebe Tante, lieber Onkel. Meinen an Euch vor 8 Tagen
geschriebenen Brief lasse ich gleich eine Karte
nachfolgen, da ich jetzt eine andere genaue
Anschrift habe. Wenn ihr schreiben solltet, dann
nur an diese Adresse. So wünsche ich Euch
allen alles gute Euer Neffe Harry Rödel.

100

The old CCC facility at Camp Skokie was reactivated during the war; the 740th Military Police unit was stationed there. One of its missions was to provide bodyguards for celebrities visiting Chicago to participate in war bond drives. The unit's band was under the direction of conductor Maj. Wayne King. During the warm months, residents of east Glenview were sometimes treated to a concert as the musicians rehearsed in a picnic shelter off Harms Road at Old Orchard Road.

Wayne King was an established big band leader before the war. At age 41, he volunteered for military service when the war broke out. He was assigned to the army specialist corps as a music officer. Widely acclaimed as "the Waltz King," he reestablished his band following the war and performed many years thereafter.

During the war, the Swain Nelson Company buildings and greenhouses were converted into a manufacturing plant for the war effort. Among the products were the components for manufacture of bombsights. Three shifts per day kept the plant humming. Women, men who were too old to serve in the military, as well as those whose medical problems made them exempt from service, worked there. Some of the workers got together for this photograph, in which they are lined up in a V (for victory) formation. The plant was so efficient that it received several E (excellence) awards for its work for the military.

Among the many ways the townspeople supported the war effort was through war bond drives. A civil defense unit was formed in anticipation of enemy attack, either from the air or on the ground. The annual Glenview Days celebration in 1942 included a briefing from local air raid warden Glenn Price. The system worked like this: an alert would be flashed from a military source, and then an alarm sounded from police and civil defense sirens. A complete blackout of the village was expected to be accomplished in 30 minutes. Fire Chief Carl Ladendorf and a team of firemen demonstrated the effects of a magnesium electron fire bomb. In an emergency, the women's division was designated to be in charge of first aid.

The school board elected to demolish the old Rugen School when the navy expanded the air station in 1942. Old school districts 32, 33, and 43 combined to form District 34 that same year. It was necessary to build a new school to replace the demolished one; the new Rugen school, shown here, opened in 1943.

As school enrollment grew by leaps and bounds, it was clear that new schools would be needed as soon as building materials became available again after the war. Between 1948 and 1961, five new elementary schools were built: Lyon, Westbrook, Hoffman, Henking, and Pleasant Ridge. In 1954, Glenview Junior High School (later renamed Springman) was constructed.

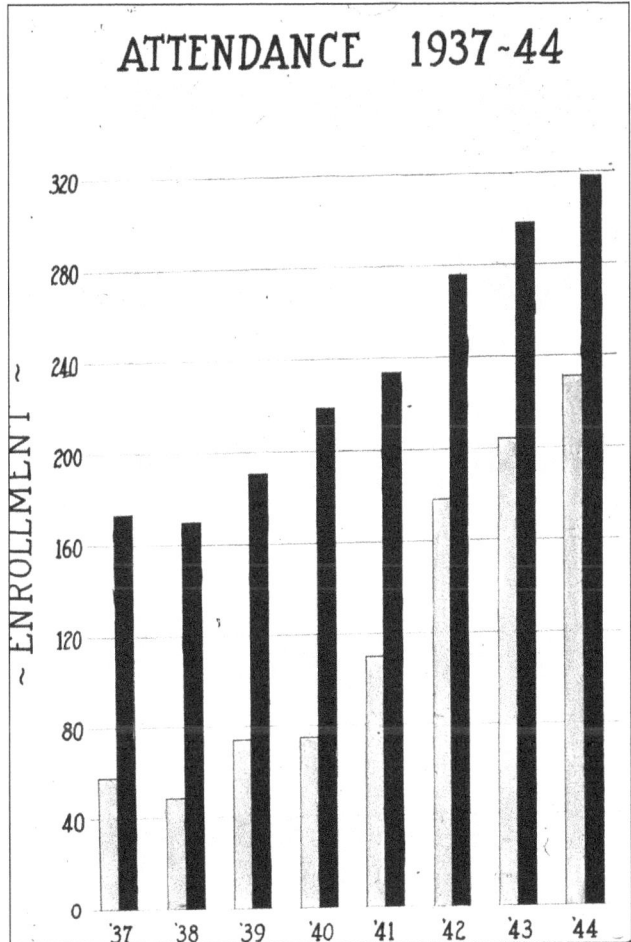

ATTENDANCE 1937~44

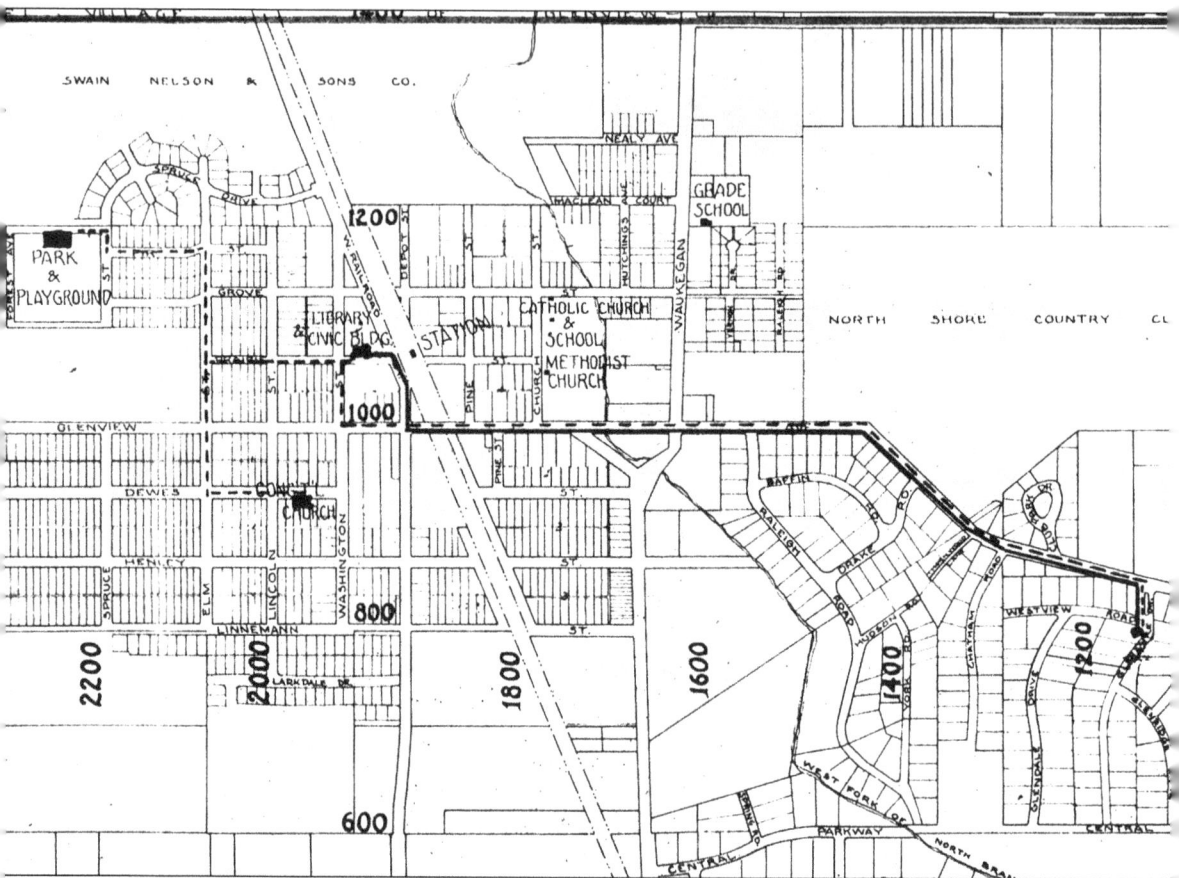

This 1940s map of Glenview demonstrates village limits when the population was about 2,500. Lake Avenue formed the village's northern boundary. At the time, Lake Street ended at Waukegan Road.

Postwar construction was evident throughout Glenview. These shops along Waukegan Road between Maplewood Lane and MacLean Court are still occupied today. (Courtesy of the Zander collection.)

Under construction on Waukegan Road at MacLean Court is the American Legion building, which also provided space for stores. The American Legion ultimately gave up the space, and stores and shops took over. (Courtesy of the Zander collection.)

Glenview Community Church traces its origins to 1897, when the Congregational Church was housed in this small frame building on Dewes Street. It was not until after World War II that a new sanctuary could be built at Elm Street and Glenview Road. The old building was converted into a residence, which is still occupied today.

Placed by the chamber of commerce, this rustic sign welcomed visitors to Glenview in 1945.

In 1946, Naval Air Station Glenview became the headquarters of naval and marine air reserve training. As the town expanded and new neighborhoods grew ever closer to the perimeter of the base, many Glenview citizens were concerned about the proximity of military flights.

The postwar building boom included a modern facility for the all-volunteer fire company in 1948.

Five

PROGRESS

At mid-20th century, about 6,000 people were living within village boundaries; that number would more than quadruple to nearly 25,000 by 1970. David Smart produced Coronet educational films in his studios on Long Valley Road in the late 1940s and 1950s. In 1957, Chicago newspaperman Jack Mabley was elected village president, and Norma Morrison was the first woman to serve on Glenview's board of trustees. The traditionally conservative community wrestled with unprecedented growth and its attendant issues. Potential expansion of the naval air station into a prestigious neighborhood triggered a successful effort to stop the plan. The Glenkirk Association for Retarded Children was chartered in 1952; the group opened its first school on Harlem Avenue in 1956. On December 31, 1957, marine pilot William P. Byrne (husband of future Chicago mayor Jane Byrne) crashed in Sunset Memorial Cemetery adjacent to the air station. Glenview architect Clarence Dahlquist's vision of a uniform Georgian Colonial design for village public buildings met with mixed success. Klipper's toy store on Waukegan Road was a source of joy for a generation of Glenview kids, and families shopped for school clothing at Dell's Apparel at Greenwood Avenue and Glenview Road. In 1957, the park district launched a leisure-time program for senior citizens. Good schools, an outstanding park district, a hometown atmosphere, and reasonable taxes drew families to the village. Glenview maintained an ambiance of a "village of homes and gardens," which would endure until the air station's closure and redevelopment at the end of the 20th century.

ST. DAVID EPISCOPAL CHURCH

As soon as building materials became available after World War II, members of St. David's Mission set about raising funds for a church. An acre of the Swain Nelson Landscape Company property was purchased, and construction of the church was finished in time for services on Christmas Eve 1946. Today St. David's Episcopal Church has expanded several times.

As life returned to normal after the war, Glenview Days parades brought enjoyment to children of all ages.

The 1929 four-room Our Lady of Perpetual Help Catholic School was constructed of red brick and located south of the church. In 1955, the school was expanded to include new classrooms, a swimming pool, and a roller rink/gymnasium. The recreation portion of the building was called the Playdium and still serves the community. The parish outgrew the old redbrick church, replacing it with the current spacious one in 1953.

Countless numbers of children of all faiths honed their skating skills at the Playdium's roller rink. This photograph shows Ted Day at the Hammond organ providing music for skaters.

As this 1965 view of the intersection of Waukegan and Glenview Roads demonstrates, the volume of traffic had increased remarkably as the postwar population continued to climb. Christmas shoppers had to be very careful as they crossed the busy streets.

Located in the heart of downtown Glenview, the war memorial was dedicated in May 1958. The war memorial committee was comprised of the American Legion Post 166, Veterans of Foreign Wars (VFW) Post 8859, and several Glenview garden clubs. The VFW post also donated the flagpole. Today the tablet includes names of those from the village who lost their lives during World War I, World War II, Korea, Vietnam, and the Iraq war. (Photograph by Bill Dawson.)

In 1954, members of VFW Post 8859 purchased the Fort, a gambling joint located on Chestnut Avenue east of Naval Air Station Glenview. The property was surrounded by a seven-foot fence. The name fit its design; there were doors with peepholes, secret rooms, a two-ton safe, and several electric buzzers to signal an impending raid. Built in 1940 and owned by the Chicago syndicate, it was run by Rocco Fischetti, a cousin of Al Capone. In 1959, a fire destroyed the place, including a six-room upstairs apartment. Robert Walsh, who served as caretaker for the VFW, occupied the apartment, along with his wife and five children. All escaped without injury.

Glenview's VFW post was named for Robert C. Ostdick, who lost his life during the Battle of the Bulge in 1944.

Brothers Hank and Ed Lange opened the Arc Restaurant and Lounge in 1948, located at Waukegan Road and Chestnut Avenue. Its Quonset hut design was a familiar sight. It was demolished in 1984 to make way for a strip mall.

Fifty years ago, the intersection of Waukegan Road and Lake Avenue had a very different look from today.

By the 1950s, the Glenview Road business district had changed little. Levernier's Grocery had supplanted the Royal Blue, and the A&P had moved to the southwest corner of Lehigh Avenue and Glenview Road.

Before the era of farmer's markets, fresh produce was available at farm stands. Heppner's, located on Glenview Road east of Harms Road, was one of the last to serve the village.

An aerial view of Glenview's downtown shows the Playdium, Patio Shops, and Colonial Court. Many old homes in the neighborhood are now gone, making way for new businesses.

In the 1950s, the southwest corner of Glenview and Waukegan Roads included the real estate offices of Wyatt and Coons on the corner, with a bakery in the middle of the block. Today a condominium and retail complex occupies the site.

In October 1961, Ed and Norma Koenig, along with Norma's brother, Tom Strey, founded the real estate agency Koenig and Strey on the northeast corner of Glenview and Waukegan Roads. Although now under the auspices of another firm, the business remains at that location today.

The west half of the old Blue Heron building remains at its original location today. Now an antiques store, it was home to Alyce's Bridal Shop for many years. A unique feature of the building's east-facing exterior is a door that appears to have been cut through a fireplace.

The Patio Shops were added to the downtown business district in the 1950s. Among the businesses located there were Chip's Casuals for men and Chicks 'n Chaps children's wear.

A cherished destination for generations of Glenview children is the Dairy Bar. It celebrated its grand opening in 1955. It is still a favorite warm-weather spot for young and old alike.

As Glenview's population grew, the need for space to process its mail did also. The new post office opened on Prairie Street in 1954. Fifty-three years later, it would be replaced again.

Carl Renneckar moved his drugstore to Glenview from Wilmette in the 1930s. In 1960, the pharmacy burned in a spectacular fire that gutted the shop. He elected to build a new store to the north at the corner of Pine Street and Glenview Road. The burned-out space was rebuilt; a hobby shop stands there today. Carl Renneckar served as village president from 1941 until 1949.

Among the businesses that have been in the community for 50 years or more is school textbook publisher Scott Foresman. Prior to moving into this new facility in 1966, the business was located in Chicago. The company received its charter from the State of Illinois in 1896. Perhaps its most famous publication ever was the Dick and Jane series of readers for young children.

Glenview students finally had a high school of their own when Glenbrook South opened in 1964. Since then, the campus has expanded and changed many times. Over the years, the Fightin' Titans have excelled in academics, music, and sports.

From the time Glenview Public Library opened its doors in the old civic building in March 1931, Glenview citizens have enjoyed access to a fine library system. The present building dates from 1955, with additions added thereafter. The Maynard family, residents of Swedenborg Park, led the effort to establish the initial library; the large public meeting room in the current facility was named in the family's honor.

Glenview's old wooden train station, which served the village for nearly a century, was replaced by this small brick one around 1960. Functional but considered by some to be nondescript, it was demolished about 30 years later, and the present one was dedicated in 1995.

In 1965, Glenview was in the Hollywood news when tragedy stuck while actress Linda Darnell was visiting the Carriage Hill home of her former secretary. The town house caught fire in the early hours of April 9. Everyone except Darnell escaped. The 43-year-old film star suffered severe burns and died the next day in Chicago's Cook County Hospital. A memorial service was held at Glenview Community Church, with the Reverend Kenneth Nye officiating.

Death of Actress Ruled Accidental

Actress Linda Darnell's death in an Apr. 9 Glenview fire was ruled accidental yesterday by a coroner's jury.

The decision came after a hear-ing

Along with the rest of the world, Glenview was excited about space travel in the 1960s. Following the first moon landing, the village board of trustees voted in July 1969 to designate the Apollo 11 astronauts, Neil Armstrong, Edwin Aldrin, and Michael Collins, honorary citizens of Glenview.

When Roosevelt Park Pool opened in 1940, it was one of the first outdoor swimming pools in the area. By 1969, it must have seemed to most kids (and their parents) the village's crowning achievement during the first 70 years following incorporation.

Visit us at
arcadiapublishing.com

www.ingramcontent.com/pod-product-compliance
Lightning Source LLC
Chambersburg PA
CBHW050627110426
42813CB00007B/1735